Book: The Sequel

el Book: The Sequel **BOOK: The Sequel** B
OOK: THE SEQUEL Book: The Sequel F
Book: The Sequel Book: The Sequel BOOK:
Book: The Sequel *Book: The Sequel* Boc
ık: The Sequel **Book:** The Sequel Book: The Se
uel **Book: The Sequel** BOOK: THE SEQUEL Boc
Book: The Sequel Book: The Sequel I
Book: The Sequel **Book: The Sequel** Book:
Book: The Sequel Book: The Sequel Boo
ok: The Sequel Book: The Sequel BC
OOK: THE SEQUEL Book: The Sequel **Book: T**

Book: The Sequel

First Lines From the Classics of the
Future by Inventive Imposters

Edited by
CLIVE PRIDDLE

PUBLIC AFFAIRS
New York

PublicAffairs books are available at special discounts for bulk purchases in the
U.S. by corporations, institutions, and other organizations. For more
information, please contact the Special Markets Department at the Perseus
Books Group, 2300 Chestnut Street, Suite 200, Philadelphia, PA 19103, call
(800) 810-4145, ext. 5000, or e-mail special.markets@perseusbooks.com.

Designed by Timm Bryson

Created with the TeleScope Publishing Platform by North Plains Systems,
Inc. (www.northplains.com)

The royalties from *Book: The Sequel* are being donated to The National Book
Foundation, presenter of the National Book Awards.

Cataloging-in-Publication Data available from the Library of Congress.

Library of Congress Control Number: 2009929790

ISBN 978-0-7867-4781-8

First Edition
10 9 8 7 6 5 4 3 2 1

CONTENTS

ON THE MAKING OF SEQUELS

Geoffrey Nunberg

Cide Hamete Benengeli recounts in the second part of this history, which concerns Don Quixote's third sally, that the priest and the barber went almost a month without seeing him, so as not to revive past events and bring them back into his memory.

—Cervantes, opening sentence of *Don Quixote*, Part 2

We are all like Scheherazade's husband, in that we want to know what happened next.

—E. M. Forster, *Aspects of the Novel*

"It is the fate of sequels to disappoint the expectations of those that have waited for them." So wrote Robert Louis Stevenson—as it happened, prophetically—in his dedication of the novel *Gatriona*, a sequel to the wildly popular *Kidnapped*, which had appeared seven years earlier. In a way, the point follows from the logic of natural selection. It's only the most successful books that get sequels, by and large, so the odds are stacked against an author's being able to duplicate the earlier achievement. Often, in fact, the author is well advised not to try. Stevenson might have left well enough alone after *Kidnapped*, Defoe after *Robinson Crusoe*, Alcott after *Little Women*, Huxley after *Brave New World*. On the other hand, think what we would have missed out on if all authors had been reluctant to expand on their past successes: no Part 2 of *Don Quixote*, no *Marriage of Figaro*, no *Through the Looking-Glass*, no *Zuckerman Unbound*. We'd have to forgo the best parts of Trollope and Balzac, not to mention the prolonged companionship of Horatio Hornblower and Harry Potter.

In any case, that sense of incompletion follows from the nature of the novel itself. However satisfying and decisive the resolution of the conflict, the ending of the story leaves us wistful. As G. K. Chesterton said, "A story can never be too long, for its conclusion is merely to be deplored, like the last halfpenny or the last pipelight." And if the characters and scene are engaging, we want to continue our acquaintance with them.

Tradition holds that Queen Elizabeth was so taken with *Henry IV* that she commanded Shakespeare to write a sequel that would show Falstaff in love, the result being *The Merry Wives of Windsor*. I'm told that tradition has probably got this story wrong, but we can all understand why a spectator would crave more of Falstaff, just as readers have craved more of Elizabeth Bennet, Heathcliff, and James Bond. And since unlike Queen Elizabeth, we're not in a position to command a continuation, we can only throw ourselves on the mercy of the author or, failing that, of an obliging artisan who will take up where the author left off, with or without permission. (It's said that Cervantes was so indignant over the appearance of a pseudonymous sequel to the first part of *Don Quixote* that when he came to write the second part, he made sure to kill his hero off at the end, rather than allowing him a tranquil old age, so as to forestall the possibility of other unauthorized versions—to no avail, it goes without saying.)

Hence the insatiable appetite for more recent news of our heroes and heroines, as witness the stupefying number of spinoffs of *Pride and Prejudice* (*Mr. Darcy's Daughters, Mrs. Darcy's Dilemma, A Letter from Lady Catherine, Affinity and Affection, Postscript from Pemberley*). And hence, too, the modern urge to redress the slights and injustices that characters have suffered at the hands of authors burdened by unexamined preconceptions and antiquated prejudices. Jean Rhys pioneered the genre in *The Wide Sargasso Sea*—really a prequel to *Jane Eyre*—which took up the cause of the first Mrs. Rochester, the madwoman in the attic. *Foe*, J. M. Coetzee's anticolonialist retelling of *Robinson Crusoe*; Alice Randall's *The Wind Done Gone*; Peter Carey's *Jack Maggs*, which reworks *Great Expectations* from the point of view of the convict Magwitch—recent fiction has shown just how many changes can be rung on this theme.

But however deadpan their tone, these exercises are never far from the preposterous. Once we give ourselves license to reinvent a story—extending it, revising it, altering its voice or point of view, wrenching it out of its time and place—we also unleash all the comic possibilities of travesty ("A literary composition which aims at exciting laughter by burlesque and ludicrous treatment of a serious work," as the *Oxford English Dictionary* puts it). And as this book demonstrates, travesty can be a highly economical effect: If it can take 250 pages to make a sequel sound plausible, a mere sentence can suffice to make it sound absurd, deftly skewering a book's pretensions—or our own. In their way, these one-sentence sequels are as affectionate about the works they start with as all those soppy reimaginings of Pemberley. They're just a lot funnier.

PART I

Animalia

The sun rose hot and dry over the Lennie Small Memorial Petting Zoo where grimy-faced children lined up to touch the rabbits.

—From *Of Man and Mouse*
(sequel to *Of Mice and Men* by John Steinbeck)
Debra Ginsberg

I'm a reliable witness, you're a reliable witness, practically all God's children are reliable witnesses—but we're none of us properly attentive to anything until we're halfway through our second cup of coffee.

—From *The Kraken Has Breakfast*
(sequel to *The Kraken Wakes* by John Wyndham)
Bridget Norman, UK

Though the island had been cleared of the Japanese, could the near weekly disappearance of a GI and the occasional discovery of furball-like deposits in the forest mean that an even more wily enemy remained?

—From *The Thin Red Lion*
(sequel to *The Thin Red Line* by James Jones)
Ned Coates, Cogan Station, PA

The sun rose hot and dry over the Lennie Small Memorial Petting Zoo where grimy-faced children lined up to touch the rabbits.

John Steinbeck

Ishmael? Shmishmael! I was big, I was white, and the ocean was mine.

—From *Moby Dick II: The Reckoning*
(sequel to *Moby Dick* by Herman Melville)
Peter Knutson

Christian the Lion finally admitted he was gay, but luckily, in a pride of lions, a gay pride member was always welcome.

—From *Christian the Lion Comes Out* (sequel to *A Lion Called Christian: The True Story of the Remarkable Bond Between Two Friends and a Lion* by Sir Anthony Bourke, John Rendall, and George Adamson)
Anonymous

I cannot remember whether I spent six hours and six minutes in the belly of the whale when I was twelve or whether I spent twelve hours and twelve minutes there when I was six.

—From *A Child's Christmas in Whales*, by Jonah Thomas (sequel to *A Child's Christmas in Wales* by Dylan Thomas)
Dianne Peeling, Allenwood, PA

"Watson," cried my great friend Sherlock Holmes, as he held aloft the chewed remains of the Persian slipper in which he had hitherto stored his shag tobacco, "you see before you all the earmarks of a dog that barks in the night. Quick, Watson! The rolled-up newspaper! The game's afoot!"

—From *The Pup of the Baskervilles* (sequel to *The Hound of the Baskervilles* by Arthur Conan Doyle)
Alexandra Mullen, Norwalk, CT

The great fish moved silently through the night water, hoping to get some fiber in its diet.

—From *Jaws: Deep Constipation*
(sequel to *Jaws* by Peter Benchley)
Jeremy Wagner, Struggling Novelist, Waukegan, IL

All animals are equal, except those with swine flu.

—From *Mexican Animal Farm*
(sequel to *Animal Farm* by George Orwell)
Agustina Casal, New York

As I lay squeezed between a tiger, an elephant, a polar bear, a velociraptor, a mound of flesh-eating bacteria and a black mamba, I couldn't help but wonder why the hell I got on another boat full of random zoo animals crossing the Pacific.

—From *Life of Pi, Part Two: An Even Smaller Lifeboat with a Larger Surety of Death* (sequel to *Life of Pi* by Yann Martel)
Scott Michonski

On most days I go just outside the window of the Oval Office, but nothing gives me greater pleasure than to mess with the newly planted arugula.

—From *The Audacity of Poop* by Bo Obama
(sequel to *The Audacity of Hope*)
Clive Joyce, BEA

PART II

Plunging into Politics

Obama, light of our hope, fire of our minds.
Our dream, our destiny. O-ba-ma.
—From *Obama* (sequel to *Lolita* by Vladimir Nabokov)
Tariqah Adams

Although I have said that a prince may rise to power in two ways, and neither of which can be entirely attributed to fortune or genius, I was not aware of who George W. Bush was at the time.

—From *Obama*
(sequel to *The Prince* by Niccolò Machiavelli)
Antonio Fasciano, New York

It is a truth universally acknowledged, that a single man who has lost his fortune in a Ponzi scheme, his job in structured finance and his retirement savings in toxic assets, must be in want of a wife.

—From *Busted and Bailed Out*
(sequel to *Pride and Prejudice* by Jane Austen)
Liz Goldenberg, New York City

Given the poor sales of my memoir, I've decidered that the American peoples, who have a great curiousness regardless my great marriage to Laura, and how I am a masterpiece of the art of marriage, and so I've written this authoritarian guide to my authoritarian marriage.

> —From *Marriage: An Authoritarian Guide*
> (sequel to *As Yet Untitled George W. Bush Memoir*
> by George W. Bush)
> Glenn Yeffeth, Publisher

"What, you only got me one stinkin' pearl?"

> —From *The "Generation Me" Pearl*
> (sequel to *The Pearl* by John Steinbeck)
> Marilyn Peake, Author

For Sale: Bank foreclosure. Quaint New England fixer-upper "to die for," featuring over half a dozen bewitching architectural roofing details.

> —From *The House of the Seven Mortgages*
> (sequel to *The House of the Seven Gables*
> by Nathaniel Hawthorne)
> Anonymous

Tom opened the white envelope and stared at the row of zeros, his rheumy eyes adjusting to the bright light shining on the glossy paper, and he realized that he had nothing, nothing was left of the treasure, that old Judge Thatcher had invested the money with that sneaky-eyed fellow with the fancy apartment, the houses in Palm Beach and France, the thousand-dollar suite, and now it was gone, all gone, and there was nothing to be done but tell Huck, tell him that they were done for, and were going back, back again to live with Aunt Polly, and to once more paint that awful fence.

—From *Hannibal, Oh Hannibal: Life on the Mississippi*
(sequel to *The Adventures of Tom Sawyer* by Mark Twain)
Evan Charkes, New York

While competition is at the core of the success of firms, it takes creativity to achieve true and memorable failure.

—From *Competitive Disadvantage*
(sequel to *Competitive Advantage* by Michael Porter)
Andrew Marrus

These white people are crazy.

—From *The Sound and the Fury: Dilsey's Story*
(sequel to *The Sound and Fury* by William Faulkner)
Debra Ginsberg, San Diego

Well, working men of the world, you united, and judging from what happened in China and Russia, I would say that maybe it wasn't such a good idea after all.

—From *The Communist Rescinding*
(sequel to *The Communist Manifesto* by Karl Marx)
Dena Kronfeld, New York City

The Magic Tree House is sold at auction after its owners grow up and face foreclosure.

—From *The Magic Fixer-Upper*
(sequel to *The Magic Tree House series*
by Mary Pope Osborne)
Marilyn Peake, Author

Ten years later, there were still Bobos—refurbished, newly enlightened, politically self-congratulatory, Bobos 2.0, if you will—but paradise wasn't what it was.

—From *Bobos Still in Paradise: How the Upper Class Remains on Top (Even with a Few Less Lattes)*
(sequel to *Bobos [Bourgeois Bohemians] in Paradise* by David Brooks)
Michael J. Agovino, Writer/Editor, New York City

Feeling triumphant, the cab driver leaned over to speak to his latest passenger, fresh off the plane: "Bet you never thought you'd be on your way to a city where the bankers are reformed characters sorting clothes for the homeless."

—From *First Try the Triborough*
(sequel to *Last Exit to Brooklyn* by Hubert Selby, Jr.)
Catheryn Kilgarriff, Publisher, London

John and Dagny stood at the front of a raging crowd and realized suddenly that, though poverty and widespread violence had illustrated the dangers of corrupt power and the praise of mediocrity, though destruction and hysteria had clearly shown the error of seeking self-sacrifice as salvation, and though John had executed a detailed and all-encompassing plan of action deftly, people were still lazy assholes who just wanted a free meal.

—From *Atlas Considers Shrugging Again*
(sequel to *Atlas Shrugged* by Ayn Rand)
Catherine McKinney

The sun, how it did shine
The swine they want to play
So we ran to the pig pen
Don't make us sick we pray.

—From *A Pig in the Wig*
(sequel to *The Cat in the Hat* by Dr. Seuss)
Becky Hall, Nursing

The IPO for Animal Agricultural Industries had gone extremely well; the pigs were now even more equal.

—From *Animal Agricultural Industries*
(sequel to *Animal Farm* by George Orwell)
Mori Irvine

At the beginning of July, during a spell of exceptionally beautiful weather, towards evening, a certain middle-aged man came down on to the street from the luxury Manhattan high-rise co-op, and slowly, almost hesitantly, set off to B-n Bridge; a morbid sense of fear, of which he was ashamed, started him thinking strangely, "if I foreclose on this apartment, my tenants will kill me!"

—From *Rent and Redemption*
(sequel to *Crime and Punishment* by Fyodor Dostoyevsky)
Barbara Abolafia, English Instructor, New Jersey

I am always drawn back to places where I have lived, the houses and their neighborhoods; for instance, there is a warehouse in Bushwick where, in the late years of the real estate bubble, I had my first New York apartment.

—From *Breakfast at Tiffany's 2*
(sequel to *Breakfast at Tiffany's* by Truman Capote)
Johannes Muentinga, Architect

I am always drawn back to places where I have lived, the houses and their neighborhoods; for instance, there is a warehouse in Bushwick, where, in the late years of the real estate bubble, I had my first New York apartment.

Truman Capote

15

Gregor Samsa awoke one morning to find that his chronic metamorphosisitis had worsened, transforming him from a giant cockroach into an HMO executive.

—From *The Metamorphosis II: Another Step Down*
(sequel to *The Metamorphosis* by Franz Kafka)
Turk Regan

I am an American all right—no job, my house is upside down on the mortgage, my credit cards canceled, my car repossessed, and my wife is leaving me to join a sustainability community upstate—but I don't care, I still have Chicago, my El, my Cubbies, and my oh my, I've got my wits, and I can still take a punch, and I'm coming back, not to worry, I am alive.

—From *The Comeback of Augie March*
(sequel to *The Adventures of Augie March*
by Saul Bellow)
Evan Charkes, New York

We were shocked that there was such a huge uproar after the bank repossessed the Witch's castle and sold the entire herd of flying monkeys to Japan for sushi.

—From *Unwanted*
(sequel to *The Wonderful Wizard of Oz* by L. Frank Baum)
Marsha Childress, Brentwood, TN

The president was pleased with his new education bill, in which students with good grades would be swept to Heaven in the Rapture, while poor performers would be kept back to repeat a grade and suffer eternal damnation.

—From *No Child Left Behind*
(sequel to *Left Behind* by Tim LaHaye and Jerry B. Jenkins)
Larry Hughes, Book Flack At Large

When I returned to Alexandria to find Justine in a burka and Narouz wearing a turban and a long beard, I became suspicious that Nessim and his friends were up to something; no one, after all, had heard in those days of the Muslim Brotherhood.

—From *The Second Book of Balthazar*,
the Alexandria Quintet (sequel to *The Alexandria Quartet* by Lawrence Durrell)
Anonymous

Howard Roark laughed. He'd known all along that no "collective of architects," no "group think" would create workable plans to rebuild in the footprint of the World Trade Towers. Now they had come to him.

—From *The Roarkscaper*
(sequel to *The Fountainhead* by Ayn Rand)
M.J. Rose, Author/Marketer, Connecticut

Those who strive to obtain great fortune are familiar with such material possessions as they hold most "precious," or in which they take most delight; whence one often sees people of "wealth" with luxury autos, fine jewelry, high-end fashions and sophisticated attitudes; those with the greatest wealth need no such desires.

—From *The Wall Street Prince*
(sequel to *The Prince* by Niccolò Machiavelli)
Daniel Radmanovic, New York

It was June 2009, and the restroom was far from the ninth tee of the KGA Golf Club in downtown Bangalore, my playing partner, the Sultan of Brunei, pointed out to me.

—From *The World is Hot, Flat, Crowded and There's a Long Line to the Bathroom* (sequel to *The World Is Flat; and Hot, Flat, and Crowded* by Thomas L. Friedman)
David Patterson, New York City

"Explain this foreclosure thing to me again?" asked Charles as he signed the lease.

—From *Brideshead Re-Revisited*
(sequel to *Brideshead Revisited* by Evelyn Waugh)
Halli Melnitsky, Editorial Assistant

In the clear afternoon light on September 10 in the cigar smoke of the Oval Office, "George, let's go over this one more time—on second thought, don't worry about a thing," Dick said in his stern, gravelly voice.

—From *The Unedited Report on 911*
(sequel to *The Report on 911* by U.S. Goverment)
Anonymous

In my younger and more vulnerable years my father gave me some advice that I've been turning over in my mind ever since. "Whenever you feel like criticizing the government," he told me, "just remember that all the taxpayers in this land haven't had the bailouts that you've had."

—From *The Great Bailout*
(sequel to *The Great Gatsby* by F. Scott Fitzgerald)
Anonymous

To the hills of golden grass with the here and there sporadic spurt of deep green trees, the bubble expanded slyly and it did not scar the valley, as nature's hand at times had, but a bubble's nature is fragile, and is destined to pop at some point.

—From *The Silicon of Sloth*
(sequel to *The Grapes of Wrath* by John Steinbeck)
Anonymous

After the death of Jay Gatsby, Daisy and Tom Buchanan, unchastened by the terrible tragedies they had wrought, continued their unfettered lives in The Eggs, where, in November, 1938, their son Pat was born.

—From *The Great Patsby*
(sequel to *The Great Gatsby* by F. Scott Fitzgerald)
Harold Augenbraum, Executive Director,
National Book Foundation

In the sunny, 73-degree late afternoon of April 17, 1969, as he had on 22 of the previous 25 days, Lyndon Johnson, the 36th president of the United States, tapped a white Keds sneaker against the rubber-coated gas pedal and slowly steered the cart—a retirement gift from Mike Mansfield, the Senate majority leader—from the LBJ ranch's pool back to his nearby residence.

—From *The Retirement Years (The Years of Lyndon Johnson, Volume 5)*. (sequel to *The Years of Lyndon Johnson, vols. 1-3* by Robert A. Caro)

Michael Schaffer, Journalist, Philadelphia

All that stuff about "value," further research shows to be irrelevant. Just buy everything, with leverage.

—From *Securities Analysis: A Modern Approach* (sequel to *Securities Analysis* by Graham and Dodd)

Ben Heller

David Paterson couldn't wait to reach Silda with the news that would hopefully send him home—Onondaga and Herkimer counties would go for Eliot in a heartbeat.

—From *Eat, Pray, Guv: Eliot Spitzer's Spiritual Return to Albany*
(sequel to *Eat, Pray, Love* by Elizabeth Gilbert)
Saralee Rosenberg, Author

PART III

Plans Gone Wry

On a Monday morning in June 1715, five men were indicted on charges of corruption and conspiracy for defrauding the Peruvian government of thousands of dollars by failing to maintain the creaky rope bridge along the high road between Lima and Cuzco, and for passing off the aging structure as a century-old Incan relic rather than the hastily woven deathtrap it proved to be for a group of unlucky travelers the year before.

—From *Perhaps Shoddy Workmanship: A Criminal Investigation into the San Luis Rey Bridge Collapse of 1714* (sequel to *The Bridge of San Luis Rey* by Thornton Wilder) Fred W. Francis

July 7th: Kicking myself in the ass for picking the Book of Ecclesiastes to memorize. How the hell do you pronounce Qoheleth?

—From *Among the Hobos: The Road Diary of Guy Montag* (sequel to *Fahrenheit 451* by Ray Bradbury) Sarah Tereniak, Pennsylvania

`Apart from the Johnny Appleseed Festival, there is nothing remarkable about Fort Wayne.`

—From *A Passage to Indiana* (sequel to *A Passage to India* by E. M. Forster) John Middleton

Before I reveal to you the identity of Julia (her grandparents are now dead, and her other relatives have lost influence as they squandered their inheritance during the excessive 80s) I want it known that I think Meryl Streep would've played me better than Jane Fonda.

—From *Sentimento*
(sequel to *Pentimento* by Lillian Hellman)
Martin Masadao, Makati, Philippines

Rosy-fingered dawn my ass: I've got f-ing RSI and Mr. World-Traveler won't get his ass off the couch to lend a hand around here.

—From *Penelope's Pissed*
(sequel to *The Odyssey* by Homer)
Anonymous

Many beers later, as he faced the idling squad car, Aureliano Buendia, Junior, was to remember earlier that afternoon when his father took him to buy ice.

—From *One Hundred Hours of Community Service*
(sequel to *One Hundred Years of Solitude*
by Gabriel García Márquez)
David Tripp, Sales Rep, New York

I have had it with this motherf——ing tiger on this motherf——ing boat!

—From *Life of Samuel L. Jackson*
(sequel to *Life of Pi* by Yann Martel)
Halli Melnitsky, Editorial Assistant

Mr. Sherlock Holmes, while basking in the glow of a successful conclusion to the mystery at Baskerville Hall, was nonetheless hounded by a nagging thought: "Watson, what if the bitch had littered?"

—From *The Puppy of the Baskervilles* (sequel to *The Hound of the Baskervilles* by Sir Arthur Conan Doyle)
Michael Cook

Okay, okay, all that stuff you just read, I made it up—but let me tell you a great story about a panda bear!

—From *The Newer Testament*
(sequel to *The Bible* by God)
Geoff Shandler

By now you have realized that *The Secret* was a load of crap, merely an ingenious smokescreen designed to throw people off the trail of The Real Secret contained in this book.

—From *The Real Secret*
(sequel to *The Secret* by Rhonda Byrne)
Jared Logan, Comedian

PART IV

Something for the Kids

Reneesme? What in the hell were my parents thinking?

—From *Dusk* (sequel to *Breaking Dawn*
by Stephenie Meyer)
Submitted by Emily Griffin, Atlanta

Sent to his room, Max works on his advanced math problems, reads books three grade levels beyond his own, and practices throwing basketballs into the hoop on his bedroom door.

—From *No Wild Things or Imagination Here, for the Overachieving Child* (sequel to *Where the Wild Things Are* by Maurice Sendak)
Marilyn Peake, Author

On a Valentine's Day, in a hall at a school
In a town known as Leeds, underneath Liz's rule
He was drinking, enjoying a night with the boys
When Horton the elephant heard a loud noise.

—From *Horton Hears the Who*
(sequel to *Horton Hears a Who* by Dr. Seuss)
Karen Gooen

That Sam-I-Am! That Sam-I-Am! I spent
three hours on the can from those damn green
eggs and ham!

> —From *Revenge of Green Eggs and Ham*
> (sequel to *Green Eggs and Ham* by Dr. Seuss)
> Veena Srinivasa

Most computers are conglomerations (this is a long word
for bundles) of steel and wire and rubber and plastic, and
electricity and RAM and GHz and DSL, and the apple juice
you spilled down the spaces in the keyboard last Sunday.

> —From *Twitty Twitty Bang Bang*
> (sequel to *Chitty Chitty Bang Bang* by Ian Fleming)
> Robert Gray, Writer/Teacher/Bookseller

I write this sitting in the kitchen sink.

> —From *I Capture the Only Apartment in*
> *My Price Range These Days*
> (sequel to *I Capture the Castle* by Dodie Smith)
> Amy Masonis, Bookseller, Nashville

My spring break?
I don't want to talk about it.
—From *Lord of the Flies 2: Ralph's Choice* (sequel to *Lord of the Flies* by William Golding)
Ryan Chapman

"Christmas won't be Christmas without boiled custard, roast goose, eggnog, figgy pudding, and fruitcake," grumbled Jo, lounging on the sofa.
—From *Big Fat Women* (sequel to *Little Women* by Louisa May Alcott)
Lauren Gilbert, Librarian, Huntington, NY

If only my parents had given me a normal name like Susan, Betty, or Elizabeth.
—From *What Made Me What I Was: Almira Gulch's Story* (sequel to *The Wonderful Wizard of Oz* by L. Frank Baum)
Marsha Childress, Brentwood, TN

Why can't you give me the respect that I am entitled to?

—From *The Taking Tree*
(sequel to *The Giving Tree* by Shel Silverstein)
Chad Miller, New York City

"I should have known the 'birdwatching' story wouldn't hold water with the judge," Tony thought to himself, ruing the day he took the binoculars back out of his closet.

—From *Then Again, Maybe I'll Do Time in the Pen*
(sequel to *Then Again, Maybe I Won't* by Judy Blume)
Toby Wahl, New York City

That afternoon, as he faced the dodgeball firing squad, fourth-grader Aureliano Buendia (who tried and failed to get everyone to call him Lee) remembered the morning when their teacher Mrs. Jacobs took them on a field trip to the planetarium, and he discovered astronaut ice cream, and the stars.

—From *One Hundred Years Later, Solitude in School*
(sequel to *One Hundred Years of Solitude*
by Gabriel García Márquez)
Jenny Doster, New York City

Um, God? About this whole period thing?
—From *Are You Still There God? It's Me, Margaret, Again*
(sequel to *Are You There God? It's Me, Margaret*
by Judy Blume)
S. Kahn

"Bother!" said Pooh. "How can I post Twitter updates without thumbs?"
—From *Winnie-the-Pooh and the Mouse at Pooh Corner*
(sequel to *The House at Pooh Corner* by A. A. Milne)
Mary Louise Ruehr, Ravenna, OH

Once there was a fat, sleek and jolly lion who ate so much carrot stew the rabbit family became tawny, scrawny and hungry all the time.
—From *Tawny, Scrawny Lion 2: The Rabbit Revolution*
(sequel to *Tawny, Scrawny Lion* by Kathryn Jackson)
Anthony Ojeda, Brooklyn

It was only after Fern Arable and some 713 county fair attendees died of the worst swine flu pandemic in American history that Homer Zuckerman discovered Charlotte's chilling final web, which read: "Kill this pig before he kills you!"

—From *Charlotte's Web II: Wilbur's Revenge*
(sequel to *Charlotte's Web* by E. B. White)
Michael Bryant, Bellingham, WA

Are you there Spring? It's me, Margaret. We're moving today. I'm so scared God. I've never lived anywhere but sunny Los Angeles. Suppose I hate my new umbrella? Suppose everyone there has nicer rain boots? Please help me God. Don't let New Jersey be too horrible. Thank you.

—From *Are You There Spring? It's Me, Margaret* (sequel to *Are You There God? It's Me, Margaret* by Judy Blume)
Ariella Gogol

That her son had been wait-listed at All Souls preschool was not the worst news Rosemary Woodhouse ever heard, but she felt troubled nonetheless.

—From *Rosemary's Toddler*
(sequel to *Rosemary's Baby* by Ira Levin)
Anonymous

Though Hooper Humperdink was pleased to see / The biggest birthday bash ever to be, / He was still a mite sore and, frankly, pissed / To learn that he'd been last on the invitation list, / So once the fete was done and the guests had flown, / He decided to have a gala of his very own / And planned to invite everyone that he knew— / Everyone, that is, except you-know-who!

—From *Hooper Humperdink's Even Bigger Bash*
(sequel to *Hooper Humperdink ... ? Not Him!* by Dr. Seuss)
Laura Martone, Guidebook Author

This is still my favorite book. And nope, I still haven't read a single word. By this time, I'm sure you're wondering whether or not I'm capable of reading. And you'd be right to wonder. Inigo often wondered the same thing about Fezzik ...

—From *The Princess Wife*
(sequel to *The Princess Bride* by William Goldman)
Jamieson Wolf

"Things are going to be different," thought Emily Elizabeth.

—From *Honey I Shrunk Clifford the Big Red Dog* (sequel to *Clifford the Big Red Dog* by Norman Bridwell)
Juan Garcia, Bookseller

They'd never believed in my invisible friend, every night when I'd said, "Goodnight nobody"—but now they believed.

> —From *Goodnight Moon: The Believers* (sequel to *Goodnight Moon* by Margaret Wise Brown) Amy Zarndt

You start out with two, but the next thing you know, you have a skyfull.

> —From *Neuter Your Pets, by the Wicked Witch of the West* (sequel to *The Wonderful Wizard of Oz* by L. Frank Baum) Marsha Childress, Brentwood, TN

"When the revolution comes, you'll be the first against a wall covered with candy-flavored wallpaper!" the head Oompa-Loompa cried. His followers readied themselves for the song-and-dance sequence.

> —From *Charlie and the Class War* (sequel to *Charlie and the Chocolate Factory* by Roald Dahl) Halli Melnitsky, Editorial Assistant

One evening, after thinking it over for some time, Harold decided to go out for a California roll but didn't know where the nearest sushi joint was. ... Luckily, there was an app for that.

—From *Harold and the New Purple iPhone3G* (sequel to *Harold and the Purple Crayon* by Crockett Johnson)
Devra Newberger Speregen, Writer, East Northport, NY

Sybil Davison blah blah blah blah blah GOT LAID blah blah blah blah blah blah, blah blah blah blah blah and now turn to page 47 to read the really juicy part and see more dirty words.

—From *Pages 47, 86, 117-119: The Juiciest Parts* (sequel to *Forever* by Judy Blume)
Devra Newberger Speregen, Writer, East Northport, NY

PART V

Midlifery

In the late summer of that year, we started out with five sets of bicep curls and then moved on to weighted triceps dips.

—From *A Farewell to Flabby Arms*
(sequel to *A Farewell to Arms* by Ernest Hemingway)
Dan Ozzi, Brooklyn

In a condominium in the exclusive new gated suburb, Shire Acres, there lived a hobbit who had become extremely rich from royalties and licensing fees.

—From *Expensive Hobbit, or, To the Bank Over There and Back Again* (sequel to *The Hobbit* by J. R. R. Tolkien)
Dennis Lien, Reference Librarian, University Of Minnesota

Date: May 15, 2009. Weight: 155 pounds. Alcohol: bottle of Chardonnay. Smokes: ten. Well, here I am. Married to Mark Darcy—the man of my dreams, whatever that bloody means. The man is never home, always at the office working his arse off. But what about me? I'm stuck cleaning this sodding flat, doing the washing up, cooking dinner, taking the kids to school. Does he ever ask me what I want to do? Of course not. And now I've gotten fat from having the children and he never buys me flowers anymore. ...

—From *Bridget Jones 3: Why Did I Want to Get Married So Badly?* (sequel to *Bridget Jones's Diary* by Helen Fielding)
Alison Callahan, New York

So, after all that, I'm back in therapy.

—From *Fat, Agnostic, and Single*
(sequel to *Eat, Pray, Love* by Elizabeth Gilbert)
Lindsay Goodman, Brooklyn

Not everything happens for a reason;
sometimes it just is what it is.

—From *The Totally Random and Without Purpose Driven
Life* (sequel to *The Purpose-Driven Life* by Rick Warren)
Francine Phillips, Writer

**Harry Potter, known as the
boy who lived and lived
again, sat peering out the
Burrow window at his absurdly
named children.**

—From *Harry Potter and the Anticlimactic
Life* (sequel to *Harry Potter and the Deathly
Hallows* by J. K. Rowling)
Jenni Lind, Brooklyn

Holden looked down at his tired, weathered hands and then
back up at the empty faces who surrounded his cubicle; they
gathered to witness his breakdown, listening as he damned
each and every one of them for their sputtering phoniness.

—From *The Return of Holden Caulfield*
(sequel to *The Catcher in the Rye* by J. D. Salinger)
Antonio Fasciano, New York

OMG. It is totes so hard to erase a web presence. Now no one will hire me...

—From *"I wish they hadn't loved me so much"* by Gossip Girl, age 31 (sequel to *You Know You Love Me (A Gossip Girl Book)* by Cecily von Ziegesar)
Jaime Leifer

Reader, I divorced him—after discovering that he had not only kept his first wife, Bertha, in the attic but that he also had hidden his East London paramour in the wine cellar.

—From *Jane Rochester née Eyre* (sequel to *Jane Eyre* by Charlotte Brontë)
Margaret Lamb

He had never considered himself the type to move back home at thirty after battling cocaine addiction; nor had he ever imagined himself so boring that he no longer wanted to narrate his life as if he were watching someone else.

—From *Low Wattage, Dull Suburbs* (sequel to *Bright Lights, Big City* by Jay McInerney)
Laura Martineau, Grant Writer, Connecticut

Having drunk three martinis, danced in a fountain and wept over some new shirts. I decided to go for a drive with that clingy social climber who could not let go of his college years.

F. Scott Fitzgerald

"So I'm thinking ... five-star spa this time around?"

—From *Deliverance II: It Was Pretty Relaxing, If Overpriced, and the Facial Was Fantastic* (sequel to *Deliverance* by James Dickey) Halli Melnitsky, Editorial Assistant

Having drunk three martinis, danced in a fountain and wept over some new shirts, I decided to go for a drive with that clingy social climber who could not let go of his college years.

—From *Gatsby Was Not So Great: My Story, by Daisy Buchanan* (sequel to *The Great Gatsby* by F. Scott Fitzgerald) Douglas Clegg, Novelist

"Shut up, I'm talking."

—From *I Understand You're an Idiot* (sequel to *You Just Don't Understand* by Deborah Tannen) Andrea Clark, New York City

Once upon a time, there was a woman who discovered she had turned into the wrong person ... her mother.

> —From *Back When We Really Grew Up*
> (sequel to *Back When We Were Grownups*
> by Anne Tyler)
> Tracey Simon, Reference Librarian, Long
> Island, NY

After years of intense therapy and major dental work, I was once again just another circus clown.

> —From *Not It* (sequel to *It* by Stephen King)
> Marsha Childress, Brentwood, TN

As if you didn't get enough about me from my first book even though I said I wasn't writing my goddam autobiography or anything, my publisher wants a sequel and I really need the dough, so while I'm not going to get into where I finally graduated from high school, went to college, or got a job, and all that Rabbit Angstrom kind of crap, I've got to put something down on paper so here goes.

> —From *The Catcher in the Rye Grows Up*
> (sequel to *The Catcher in the Rye* by J. D. Salinger)
> Robert Kimzey, Montclair, NJ

Buying the Nimbus 10,000 was the first sign that something was wrong.
—From *Harry Potter and the Mid-Life Crisis* (sequel to *Harry Potter and the Deathly Hallows* by J. K. Rowling)
Kara Race-Moore

By outward appearances she seemed the picture of contented loveliness as she methodically moved her charcoal pencil across the paper, rendering yet another praiseworthy and extremely mediocre caricature of her unsuspecting subject; while inwardly her mind was diligently scheming and mapping out a precision plan for severing the "perfect" bond between them.
—From *Diminishing Bliss & Something Amiss* (sequel to *Emma* by Jane Austen)
Diana Humphrey

Last night I took an Ambien and had a good night's sleep without dreaming about Manderly.
—From *After the Fire* (sequel to *Rebecca* by Daphne du Maurier)
M. J. Rose, Author/Marketer, Connecticut

Love means apologizing when you made a mistake.

—From *Love Story: Part 2*
(sequel to *Love Story* by Erich Segal)
Elizabeth Schwebel-Wind

Sabina lay in meditation on her lounge chaise listening on her iPod to the Buddha's four noble truths when a mosquito jolted her awake—killing it with the satisfying crunch of the palm of her hand, she was equally stricken with the four ignoble truths of her situation: she was 50, pregnant, out of a job, and stranded in Guayaquil, Ecuador.

—From *The Irresistible Weight of Karenin* (sequel to *The Unbearable Lightness of Being* by Milan Kundera)
Amala Lane, Filmmaker, New York City

On second thought, maybe you should both just shut up, get a hobby, and pretend everything is okay.

—From *And Ne'er the Twain Shall Meet* (sequel to *Men Are from Mars, Women Are from Venus* by John Gray)
David Young, Sapporo, Japan

Full of vexation come I, with complaint / Against my hormones gone so far awry.

—From *A Midsummer Night's Hot Flash* (sequel to *A Midsummer Night's Dream* by William Shakespeare)
Jyotsna Sreenivasan

The day Boo Radley and I finally married, I don't imagine anyone in the whole of Maycomb County knew just what to make of it, naturally excepting Dill and Tom Robinson, who were themselves to jump the broom in the very next year.

—From *Mockingbird Falls: The Long-Awaited Sequel* (sequel to *To Kill a Mockingbird* by Harper Lee)
David Wright, Librarian, Seattle

Although tomorrow had indeed proven to be another day, it wasn't quite the day Scarlett had hoped it would be when she awoke to find herself alone, in her familiar bed at Tara, the smell of waffles and grits clinging to her nostrils, as she began to wonder which of the portieres were the prettiest to make a new dress from to re-entice her hunky husband—aka Mr. Rhett Butler—back into her life.

—From *Bringing It All Back Home* (sequel to *Gone with the Wind* by Margaret Mitchell)
Julie Hayes, St. Louis

Reader, I divorced him.

—From *The Midlife Crisis of Jane Eyre*
(sequel to *Jane Eyre* by Charlotte Brontë)
Emma Joyce

Benjamin Braddock sighed as he made one more plea: "Elaine, darling, I'd really rather not spend Mother's Day with your side of the family, this year."

—From *The Post Graduate*
(sequel to *The Graduate* by Charles Webb)
Karen Gooen

It was love at first sight. The first time Yossarian saw Sweden, he fell madly in love with it.

—From *They'll Never Catch Me: 22 Years in Scandinavia*
(sequel to *Catch 22* by Joseph Heller)
Bill Michtom, Portland, OR

I could not contain my excitement nor the buzzing in my gulliver as I thought about the evening ahead of me: bangers and beans with the missus and kids and then off with my droogs for darts at the pub.

—From *A More Clockwork Orange*
(sequel to *A Clockwork Orange* by Anthony Burgess)
Joe Coglianese, Oak Park, IL

What I meant to say was that it's okay to leave your wife if a hotter piece of ass comes along.

—From *Howard Stern: Private Parts 2,*
This Time I'm Sirius
(sequel to *Howard Stern: Private Parts* by Howard Stern)
Devra Newberger Speregen, Children's Book Author, East
Northport, NY

Slovenly, pumped Buck Mulligan came from the Stairmaster lathered in sweat, looked in the mirror, and cursed.

—From *Useless* (sequel to *Ulysses* by James Joyce)
Peter Mayer, Fiction Writer, New York City

Emma Woodhouse, handsome, clever, and rich, with a comfortable home and husband, seemed to unite all of the horrors of a too prudent marriage in her single person; and had lived nearly all of her days since her twenty-first year with nothing but distress and vexation.

—From *Emma Knightley* (sequel to *Emma* by Jane Austen)
Mary Pagones, Writer, New Jersey

.

D'Artagnan was pleased to see that his three old comrades in arms had changed little since last they met—a bit softer, perhaps, but still lively companions.

—From *The Three Musketeers: Fluffy, Not Stuffy*
(sequel to *The Three Musketeers* by Alexandre Dumas)
Larry Hughes, Book Flack At Large

Well, I still have no idea why my wife left me except that I must be deficient in a gamut of ways, another number of which I could describe to you in an intricate, detached manner.

—From *The Dog That Yelps and Then Flips Diary* (sequel to *The Wind-up Bird Chronicle* by Haruki Murakami)
Tim Mak

Gregor Samsa awoke one morning from anxious dreams to find himself transformed into his father.

—From *A More Common Metamorphosis*
(sequel to *Metamorphosis* by Franz Kafka)
Emma Joyce

"That's per hour?!"

—From *Still Kvetching: The Return of Portnoy*
(sequel to *Portnoy's Complaint* by Philip Roth)
Gary Morris, Brooklyn

Boarding the tour bus in Rego Park, our destination that
grand symbol of Americana on the endless Jersey shore, I
tugged at my leisure suit and don't you just hate the way the
kids are wearing their pants today and I looked at Dean, ever
Dean, wondering whatever became of the quarters we'd
been saving, budgeting our Social Security checks and
sharing blood pressure meds, for our pilgrimage to the
Atlantic City slots.

—From *On the Tour Bus* (sequel to
On the Road by Jack Kerouac)
Jeff Markowitz, Mystery Writer, Monmouth Junction, NJ

"Good riddance to bad rubbish," I thought as I
signed my divorce papers with my ex-wife,
Lolita.

—From *After Lolita: Lock Up Your Daughters!*
(sequel to *Lolita* by Vladimir Nabokov)
Janet Saines

Paul Harkonnen, wishing he was riding his old trusty sand worm, cursed at the string of headlights on the undulating, arid LIE.

—From *Dune: House of Hampton*
(sequel to *Dune* by Frank Herbert)
Carl Lennertz, VP, Retail Marketing, HarperCollins

In my younger and more vulnerable years my father gave me some bathtub gin that has been turning over in my liver ever since.

—From *The Great Gasby*
(sequel to *The Great Gatsby* by F. Scott Fitzgerald)
Anonymous

Before we begin, I must confess the most lamentable, but personally fortuitous, truth: Jane went crazy, too.

—From *The Third Mrs. Rochester*
(sequel to *Jane Eyre* by Charlotte Brontë)
Alison Trotta, Writer, Somewhere Near The Coffee Pot

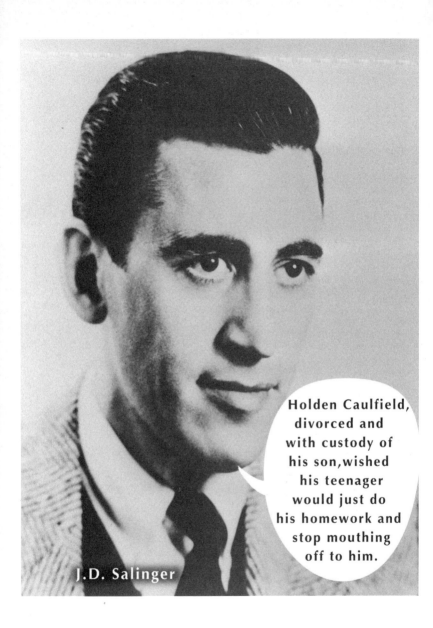

Holden Caulfield, divorced and with custody of his son, wished his teenager would just do his homework and stop mouthing off to him.

J.D. Salinger

After years of consuming rich, creamy milk chocolate, Charlie Bucket's cardiologist gave the gooey-in-his-center candyman an ultimatum: Switch to the dark stuff and start using the stairs instead of the glass elevator.

—From *Charlie and the All-Natural 80% Cocoa Dark Chocolate Factory*
(sequel to *Charlie and the Chocolate Factory* by Roald Dahl)
Lisa Safran, Writer

Holden Caulfield, divorced and with custody of his son, wished his teenager would just do his homework and stop mouthing off to him.

—From *The Catcher In the Rye: Reality Bites*
(sequel to *The Catcher in the Rye* by J. D. Salinger)
Jeremy Wagner, Struggling Novelist, Waukegan, IL

The Tin Man looked on as wife, Dorothy, cradled their baby boy for the very first time, and with his best friend the Scarecrow at his side, pondered, "He has her eyes . . . but his hair looks very strawlike."

—From *Life After Oz*
(sequel to *The Wonderful Wizard of Oz* by L. Frank Baum)
Geri DiTella, Philadelphia

The first shock was receiving an electric bill.

—From *Invisible Man Visible*
(sequel to *Invisible Man* by Ralph Ellison)
Steven G. Kellman, Professor, San Antonio, TX

Rand couldn't believe that after all he'd been through—after showing such exceptional wisdom, strength, courage, and even cunning in saving the world and the very fabric of time itself—he was still just so darn dense about women.

—From *The Dragon Retired*
(sequel to *The Gathering Storm* by Robert Jordan)
Mo Radley, Dekalb, IL

When he was nearly thirty-six, my brother Jem got his heart badly broken when his fourth marriage fell apart, mostly because his wife never could get used to Boo, who lived with them and creeped her out by making little wooden dolls of her and putting them in the hollow tree out front.

—From *To Kill a Mockingbird Part 2: Walter Cunningham Strikes Back* (sequel to *To Kill a Mockingbird* by Harper Lee)
Silas House

Max wanted to jump on the table and growl at his wife and kids, but he didn't.

—From *Too Tame* (sequel to *Where the Wild Things Are* by Maurice Sendak)
Robin Dennis, Flower Mound, TX

We were somewhere around Barstow on the edge of the desert when the ayurvedic cleansing began to take effect.

—From *Love and Inner Tranquility in Las Vegas: A Healing Spiritual Return to the Heart of the American Dream* (sequel to *Fear and Loathing in Las Vegas: A Savage Journey to the Heart of the American Dream* by Hunter S. Thompson)
Norman Szabo, Taiwan, ROC

"Tom, darling, I think it's time we replaced that bug zapper on the dock," said Daisy as she langorously stretched out on the divan. "Someone might find that green light distracting."

—From *The Banal Buchanans* (sequel to *The Great Gatsby* by F. Scott Fitzgerald)
Karen Gooen

Swiftly approaching old age, life had few mysteries left for Nancy Drew, save one—where was Ned hiding his Viagra, and how could she get him to stop taking it?

—From *The Secret of the Old Cock* (sequel to *The Secret of the Old Clock* by Carolyn Keene)
Michael Cornelius, Chambersburg, PA

PART VI

As I Lay
Undead and
Dying

Horatio: "Tis said his ghost doth walk, but I'll not
AAAAAAAAAAH—"

—From *The Tragedy of Hamlet, Zombie of Denmark*
(sequel to *The Tragedy of Hamlet, Prince of Denmark*
by William Shakespeare)
Candace Lines

I have always found wearing a motorcycle
helmet to be a tedious bore.

—From *The Eight Pillars of Wisdom*
(sequel to *The Seven Pillars of Wisdom* by T. E. Lawrence)
Kevin H. Posey

I'm in Heaven??

—From *Doubting Thomas*
(sequel to *The Bible* by God and men)
Anonymous

Susan wanted to kick him for being so stupid, wished he'd just sit up and tell her what to do; Peter was the oldest, he should be the one called on to identify Edmund and Lucy, not her—how dare he just lie there like a rag doll?

—From *After Narnia*
(sequel to *The Last Battle* by C. S. Lewis)
Deborah Green, Sydney, Australia

Yesterday I suddenly realized that my husband is a controlling, domineering, obsessive-compulsive monster.

—From *Noonish*
(sequel to *Breaking Dawn* by Stephenie Meyer)
Anonymous

Billy Pilgrim was dead, to begin with.

—From *Slaughterhouse Christmas Carol*
(sequel to *Slaughterhouse Five* by Kurt Vonnegut)
Phil Freed, Massachusetts

At night, I would lie in bed under my net, dreaming of blood.

—From *The Secret Life of Mosquitos: A Vampire Thriller*
(sequel to *The Secret Life of Bees* by Sue Monk Kidd)
Annie Scott, Writer, New York City

After picking himself up out of the dirt and vegetation, Piggy began to wander after the boys.

—From *Lord of the Flies II: Zombie*
(sequel to *Lord of the Flies* by William Golding)
Wesley Irvin

```
I died today or yesterday
maybe, I don't know.
```

—From *Stranger Remains*
(sequel to *The Stranger* by Albert Camus)
Robert Pigeon

65

Communism fell, Kantor and Grotowski died, but Polish alternative theatre, amazingly, continues to exist!

—From *Polish Alternative Theatre, the Sequel* (sequel to *Alternative Theatre in Poland, 1954-1989* by Kathleen M. Cioffi) Kathleen Cioffi

Echecrates: "Were you yourself, Phaedo, there when Socrates rose from the grave as a zombie, opening a giant can of wup ass on the citizens of Athens?" Phaedo: "Yes, Echecrates, I was—and I was AFRAID."

—From *Phaedo 2: The Revenge of Socrates* (sequel to *Phaedo* by Plato) E. J. McAdams, New York

Brains!

—From *The Great Gatsby II: The Zombie Years* (sequel to *The Great Gatsby* by F. Scott Fitzgerald) Peter Tatara, New York City

Although he could no longer see the dead, Bod still visited graveyards.

—From *Out of the Graveyard*
(sequel to *The Graveyard Book* by Neil Gaiman)
Anonymous

In the end God said, "Let there be nuclear light"; man lit the fuse and all once more was night. [Note: the great advantage of this sentence is that no more sentences are needed in the sequel.]

—From *The Bible—The Sequel [in entirety]*
(sequel to *The Bible* by Various)
Hurd Hutchins, New York City

Two households, both alike in dignity, In curs'd Verona, where we lay our scene, From ancient grudge break to new mutiny, Where civil brains makes undead hands unclean, From forth the fatal loins of these two foes, A pair of star-cross'd lovers take their unlife ...

—From *Romeo & Juliet & Zombies*
(sequel to *Romeo and Juliet* by William Shakespeare)
Brian Archibald, Virginia

John Updike

Dead six weeks now, Harry "Rabbit" Angstrom is still trying to recapture the grace of his days of human basketball court glory, but he finds that, despite what his old human nickname would suggest and despite his soul having found a new home in an actual rabbit, hopping does not quite suit him.

Before I tell you why I wore pants to heaven, I would like to tell you, or at least identify for you, how to get here in the first place.

—From *Me, Again* (sequel to *Me* by Katharine Hepburn)
Martin Masadao, Makati, Philippines

I loved being a vampire and a mother; Edward was still breathtakingly gorgeous, as always, but there was something missing—was it because I had no more breath to take?

—From *Twilight V: Broken Sunrise*
(sequel to *Twilight* by Stephenie Meyer)
Brendan McGinn, New York City

Dead six weeks now, Harry "Rabbit" Angstrom is still trying to recapture the grace of his days of human basketball court glory, but he finds that, despite what his old human nickname would suggest and despite his soul having found a new home in an actual rabbit, hopping does not quite suit him.

—From *Rabbit Reincarnated*
(sequel to *Rabbit at Rest* by John Updike)
Ben Heller

PART VII

A Quickie

There were 117 psychoanalysts on the Pan Am flight to Vienna and I had either slept with or dreamt of sleeping with at least twenty of them.

—From *Fear of Intimacy*
(sequel to *Fear of Flying* by Erica Jong)
Sherry Chancellor, Attorney, Pensacola, Fl

"Jonny," Dolores thinks to herself, staring at a handsome, dark-haired boy across her crowded classroom, "sun of my soul, inferno of my lap."

—From *Jonny* (sequel to *Lolita* by Vladimir Nabokov)
Blair Mastbaum

It was Wang Lung's marriage day, the 21st of September, and the couple danced the night away, knowing love was here to stay. ...

—From *The Good Earth, Wind and Fire Concert*
(sequel to *The Good Earth* by Pearl S. Buck)
Anonymous

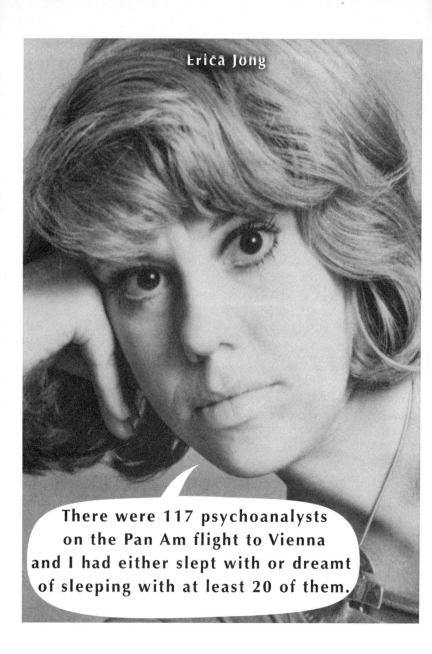

The master bedroom in the Governor's House at Port Mahon, occupied by a tall, handsome, pillowed octoroon, was filled with triumphant movement.

—From *Mistress and Commander*
(sequel to *Master and Commander* by Patrick O'Brian)
Carol Schneck, Bookseller, Okemos, MI

All of what I learned in psychoanalysis can now be found in self-help books which teach one not only how to get over a fear of flying or a fear of sex or even a fear of psychoanalysis, but also clue the reader to the latest technology—thus my fantasies of the zipless f—ck can now be achieved with Velcro!

—From *Fear of Flying Coach*
(sequel to *Fear of Flying* by Erica Jong)
G. Warlock Vance, Instructor, UNCG

Make love; not too much; mostly with people.

—From *The Omniphile's Dilemma*
(sequel to *The Omnivore's Dilemma* by Michael Pollan)
Seth Chalmer, New York City

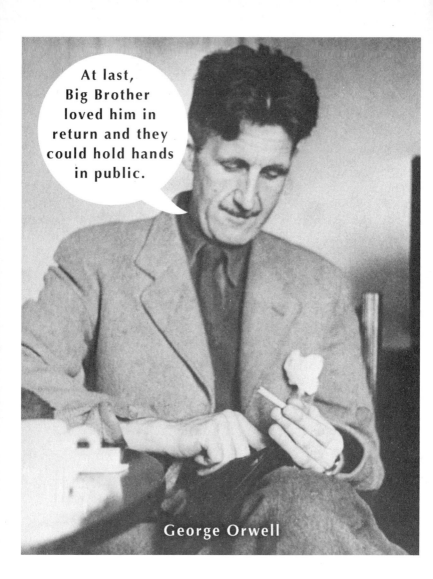

Gandalf rolled over and caressed Bilbo's hair lovingly, deeply inhaling the sweet scent of pipeweed and Astroglide.

—From *The Hobbit II: Bareback Again*
(sequel to *The Hobbit* by J. R. R. Tolkien)
Anonymous


```
At last, Big Brother loved
him in return, and they could
hold hands in public.
```
—From *1985* (sequel to *1984* by George Orwell)
Michael Laser, Montclair, NJ

PART VIII

A Truth Universally Acknowledged

It is a truth universally acknowledged, that a married woman in possession of a reasonably annoying husband must want a little something on the side.

—From *Indifference and Infidelity*
(sequel to *Pride and Prejudice* by Jane Austen)
Douglas Clegg, Novelist

It is a truth universally acknowledged that a single man in possession of a large fortune must be in want of a prenuptial agreement.

—From *Pride and Prejudice: Pemberly, Community Property*
(sequel to *Pride and Prejudice* by Jane Austen
Caitlin Fitzpatrick

It is a truth universally acknowledged that every wealthy wife must be in want of a pool boy.

—From *Real Housewives of Hertfordshire*
(sequel to *Pride and Prejudice* by Jane Austen)
Jesse Feldman

It is a truth universally acknowledged that an author who has had her most famous book dreadfully reduced by the addition of zombies to the plot, will want to effect her own revenge in the form of a lawsuit, or, failing that, a blockbuster sequel: Pride and Prejudice and Aliens.

> —From *Jane Austen Strikes Back: The Voice of the Undead Author* (sequel to *Pride and Prejudice* by Jane Austen)
> Patrice Fitzgerald, Writer, Stratford, CT

Whatever truth may be universally acknowledged by men and women married or single alike, the fact that Darcy turned out to be a priggish jackass was one Elizabeth Bennet could not escape.

> —From the sequel to *Pride and Prejudice* by Jane Austen
> Anonymous

Lizzy the Lion is tired of being the only responsible hunter in her pride, with her frivolous mother and sisters content to only sun and groom all day and encourage the males on the periphery.

> —From *Pride's Prejudice*
> (sequel to *Pride and Prejudice* by Jane Austen)
> Julianne Long, Flower Mound, TX

It is a truth universally acknowledged, that a married man in possession of a good fortune, must tire of his atrocious in-laws before the first anniversary of his nuptials.

—From *Tired and Prejudiced*
(sequel to *Pride and Prejudice* by Jane Austen)
Karen Schlosberg, Natick, MA

It is a truth universally acknowledged, that a married man in possession of a few bucks must be in want of an excuse to go out drinking with his buddies.

—From *Beer and Barhopping*
(sequel to *Pride and Prejudice* by Jane Austen)
David MacGregor, Arlington, VA

Things had been going seriously downhill since Darcy was diagnosed with Aspergers and the liquored-up Elizabeth took up mud-wrestling, but the Drug Squad raid on the Pemberley Ball was truly the final indignity.

—From *Disillusion and Rancour*
(sequel to *Pride and Prejudice* by Jane Austen)
Candida Gower, Publisher, Kent, Great Britain

It is a truth universally acknowledged that a newly married couple in possession of a good fortune must be in want of a child.

—From *Complaisance and Confinement*
(sequel to *Pride and Prejudice* by Jane Austen)
Terry Lucas, Bookseller/Librarian,
Westhampton Beach/Southampton, NY

As it turns out, bugs can live for lengthy periods of time without benefit of food. So while Gregor Samsa's family thought, much to their relief, that he had finally deteriorated, in fact, he had been quietly hibernating for months ...

—From *Metamorphing Back*
(sequel to *The Metamorphisis* by Franz Kafka)
Claudia Copquin, Freelance Journalist And Author,
Long Island, NY

As Gregor Samsa awoke one morning from uneasy dreams he found himself transformed in his bed into a gigantic car dealership.

—From the sequel to *The Metamorphosis* by Franz Kafka
Anonymous

When Gregor Samsa awoke one morning from troubled dreams, he found himself transformed in his bed into a winged, scaly, eminently merchandisable licensed character.

—From *Metamorphosis 2: Buggin' Out!*
(Disney/Hyperion)
(sequel to *Metamorphosis* by Franz Kafka)
Rob Kutner

One morning, as Gregor Samsa was waking up from anxious dreams, he discovered that in his bed he had been invented by a claims adjustor from the Worker's Accident Insurance Institute for the Kingdom of Bohemia to explain unconscious fantasies the man had about the body and family relationships based on identifications.

—From *The Meta-Metamorphosis*
(sequel to *The Metamorphosis* by Franz Kafka)
Evan Gregory, Brooklyn

One morning, as an intrusion of cockroaches awoke anxiously from a collective dream, it discovered that while sleeping it had been transformed into an identical mob of neurotic, banal, and ambition-less Eastern European males.

—From *Metamorphosis II: This Time, It's Personal*
(sequel to *The Metamorphosis* by Franz Kafka)
Angi Campbell, Writer, Washington

As Gregor Samsa awoke one morning from uneasy dreams he found himself transformed in his bed into a gigantic insect; with earnestness and great vigor he gave a sigh of relief knowing that finally he could begin the career he always wanted: pest and insect control.

—From *Kafka's Guide to Entomology*
(sequel to *The Metamorphosis* by Franz Kafka
Rachel Aubrey, Grad Student

Someone must have slandered Jamal K., for one morning, without having done anything truly wrong, he was rendered.

—From *No Trial* (sequel to *The Trial* by Franz Kafka)

Anonymous

Call me, Ishmael!

—From *Moby Dick's Guide to Dating at Sea* (sequel to *Moby Dick* by Herman Melville)

Dan Ozzi, Brooklyn

Draw near and I will tell you a tale of the one that got away.

—From *The Old Man and the Sea*, by Shlomo Ben Ishmael (sequel to *Moby Dick* by Herman Melville)

Edmund Glass

Call me Naïve, but I really hadn't anticipated the international ban on whaling and had taken the job as a Republican publicist for lack of anything else to do.

—From *Moby Dick II*
(sequel to *Moby Dick* by Herman Melville)
Michael Ricciardelli, Managing Editor,
Law School Health Refrom Blog,
Www.HealthReformWatch.com, Newark, NJ

First, catch your whale.

—From *The Idiot's Guide to Scrimshaw*, by Ishmael Smith
(sequel to *Moby Dick* by Herman Melville)
Roger Kimball

Look, the boat sank, the whale won, I'm sick of talking about it, and stop calling me Ishmael!

—From *Moby Ditto*
(sequel to *Moby Dick* by Herman Melville)
Esther Friesner

Call me a schlemiel!

—From *Moishe, The Dick*
(sequel to *Moby Dick* by Herman Melville)
Daniel Klein, Great Barrington, MA 01230

Call me a Fillet O' Fish meal.

—From *Moby Dick II: The White Whale Meets
the 60-Mile-Long Japanese Drift Net*
(sequel to *Moby Dick* by Herman Melville)
Michael Bryant, Bellingham, WA

"OK, OK already, we'll call you Ishmael ... Ishmael, you must immediately stop hunting whales in this ocean," the Greenpeace volunteer shouted through his bullhorn at the crazed sailor aboard the whale ship Pequod.

—From *Sins of the Father*
(sequel to *Moby Dick* by Herman Melville)
Marilyn Peake, Author

"Call me, Ishmael," whispered Kevin.

—From *Fire Island Shore Leave*
(sequel to *Moby Dick* by Herman Melville)
John Middleton

Call me Ishmael.

—From *A Million More Little Pieces*
(sequel to *A Million Little Pieces* by James Frey)
Rob Kutner

It turned out not to be the worst of times at all;
they got so much worse later.

—From *A Tale of Three Cities*
(sequel to *A Tale of Two Cities* by Charles Dickens)
Clive Priddle

It was a so-so time. It was a not-too-bad time.

—From *More Realistic Expectations*
(sequel to *Great Expectations* by Charles Dickens)
Robert Loy, Charleston, SC

It was the 1986 Mets; it was the 1962 Mets.

—From *A Tale of Two Teams*
(sequel to *A Tale of Two Cities* by Charles Dickens)
Lucas Rizo

It was a rockin' good time, it was a bummer, it was the age of Google, it was the age of Twitter, it was the epoch of Obama, it was the epoch of Bush, it was the season of the witch, it was the age of Aquarius, it was the spring of beer, it was the winter of Valium, we had everything before us, we had nothing before us, we were all going direct to McDonalds, we were all going direct to Whole Foods—in short, the period was so far like the last period, that some of its noisiest authorities insisted on its being received, for good or for evil, in the superlative degree of a flickering Kindle.

—From the sequel to *A Tale of Two Cities*
by Charles Dickens
Marshall TK, Ridgewood, NJ

It wasn't necessarily the best of times or the worst of times. All in all, they were just middlin' times.

—From *A Tale of Two Suburbs*
(sequel to *A Tale of Two Cities* by Charles Dickens)
Suzanne Arruda, Mystery Writer

It was the best of the New York Times, it was the worst of the New York Times.

—From *A Sale of Two Dailies*
(sequel to *A Tale of Two Cities* by Charles Dickens)
Peter Mayer, Fiction Writer, New York City

It was the most hurried of times, it was the slowest of times, it was the age of Smart Cars, it was the age of Hummers, it was the epoch of the bonus, it was the epoch of the bankrupt, it was the season of Lights, it was the season of Red, it was the spring in my seat, it was the winter of my pants, we had every car before us, we had every truck behind us, we were all going direct to work, we were all dreaming the other way—in short, the highway was so far like life, that some of its noisiest authorities insisted on this pair being ticketed, both tortoise and hare, in the super-elite lane marked "HOV only."

—From *A Tale of Two Commuters*
(sequel to *A Tale of Two Cities* by Charles Dickens)
David Jeffrey, New York City

Reader, I divorced him—I figured that tethering myself to a one-eyed man in a drafty house with no resale value wasn't the savviest of things I had done in my life.

—From *Smart Governesses Marry Money*
(sequel to *Jane Eyre* by Charlotte Brontë)
Jennifer Kasius

Reader, we had a baby.

—From *Jane's Heir*
(sequel to *Jane Eyre* by Charlotte Brontë)
Courtney Allison

In the middle, God sighed.

> —From *The Bible: God Tries Again*
> (sequel to *The Bible* by God and lots of humans)
> Allison Moore, Episcopal Priest, Fort Lee, NJ

Well, that didn't work out.

> —From *The Bible II: So Satan Won*
> (sequel to *The Bible* by God)
> Anonymous

Happy families are all alike; every unhappy family is unhappy in its own way ... like when Mom commits adultery and throws herself under a train.

> —From *Sergei Karenin's Therapy Journals*
> (sequel to *Anna Karenina* by Leo Tolstoy)
> Miriam Goderich, Literary Agent

Happy Meals are all alike; each unhappy
meal is unhappy in its own way.

—From *Anna McKarenina*
(sequel to *Anna Karenina* by Leo Tolstoy)
Rick Joyce

PART IX

Mash-Ups

Stately, ripped.

—From *Ulysses: The Complete One-Day Workout* (sequel to *Ulysses* by James Joyce)

Rob Kutner

It was 50 percent the best of times, 50 percent the worst of times, and 50 percent regular times.

—From *A Tale of Two Cities: Adaptation by Yogi Berra* (sequel to *A Tale of Two Cities* by Charles Dickens)

Annie Scott, Writer, New York City

When the third crew of decorators vanished without a trace, the producer began to think that renovating the house on Ash Tree Lane had not been such a good idea—but it did make great TV.

—From *House of Leaves: Extreme Makeover Edition* (sequel to *House of Leaves* by Mark Danielewski)

Emma Joyce

Let's face it, son of Achilles, if you do not do something about that terrible temper of yours, you will shoot yourself in the foot.

—From *Homer's Guide to Anger Management for Heroes*
(sequel to *The Iliad* by Homer)
Anonymous

Who is John Galt?

—From *I'll Take "Abstruse Books" for $1000:*
Atlas on "Jeopardy!"
(sequel to *Atlas Shrugged* by Ayn Rand)
Eric Weinstein

My family name being Rubble and my given name being Barney, my senescent tongue can make no more of both sounds than "Babble"; and so it was that I came to be ignored.

—From *Few Expectations*
(sequel to *Great Expectations* by Charles Dickens)
Terry Noble, Bay Shore, NY

At first they weren't even allowed to watch, and they would come undercover—but once they began to fight ... the women changed everything.

—From *Fight Club 2*
(sequel to *Fight Club* by Chuck Palahniuk)
Anonymous

We were somewhere around Hoboken, on the edge of the city, when the traffic began to take hold.

—From *Fear and Loathing in Manhattan*
(sequel to *Fear and Loathing in Las Vegas*
by Hunter S. Thompson)
Submitted by Peter Knox, New York City

As Roebuck Ramsden opens the morning's letters in his study, he realizes the house has become very quiet—too quiet.

—From *Man, Superman, Alien and Predator* (sequel to
Man and Superman by George Bernard Shaw)
Norman Szabo, Taiwan, ROC

One moment Khan Noonien Singh stood aboard the USS Enterprise plotting the takeover of the entire starship fleet, the next he found himself beamed through a wormhole to the front porch of of a farmhouse in Great Depression-era Oklahoma, where he was quickly beaten with a broom by Ma Joad.

—From *The Grapes of Wrath of Khan* (sequel to *The Grapes of Wrath* by John Steinbeck)

Michael Regan

Sit down, class, and get to work or, by the whale, I'll harpoon you to your seats.

—From *They Call Me Mr. Ishmael (a survivor of a doomed whale hunt goes back to the classroom to teach rowdy Londoners)* (sequel to *Moby Dick* by Herman Melville)
Suzanne Arruda, Mystery Writer

In the decade of the present century preceding its teens, and in the late evening, there drove up to the great Vegas dance club a large limousine, driven by a muscular man in a well-tailored suit, and two very inebriated women stepped out, visibly absent of underclothing

—From *People, Us, and In Touch: The Tabloids Weigh In* (sequel to Vanity Fair by William Makepeace Thackeray)
Karen Gooen

There, in the small corner of the wine cellar just behind the Cask of Amontillado, was the jewel that had been thought stolen all these years; the very stone about which the entire Capulet-Montague feud had first begun.

—From *Perchance, a Misunderstanding* (sequel to *Romeo and Juliet* by William Shakespeare)
Tsan Abrahamson, Berkeley, CA

PART X

Irony Chef

The truth is, I prefer chocolate chip.
—From *À la recherche du temps perdu: Part Deux* (sequel
to *À la recherche du temps perdu* by Marcel Proust)
Ben Strevens

Estragon, sitting at a small table and trying to take the lid off
his triple-tall, one-pump caramel, two-pump chocolate,
extra-hot, no-foam, no-fat latte, asks Vladimir, "Are you
sure he said this Starbucks and not the one across the
street?"
—From *Waiting for Godot: Starbucks Edition*
(sequel to *Waiting for Godot* by Samuel Beckett)
Traci Killen

**Last night I dreamt I burnt down
Manderley again.**
—From *Mrs. Danvers' Book of BBQ*
(sequel to *Rebecca* by Daphne du Maurier)
Ellie Tupper, Editor

Marian was tired of eating cake; she was all for feminist symbolism, but her thighs were getting fat and her pants made that annoying wooosh sound when she walked. She didn't want pearls, she wanted Jenny Craig.

—From *The Edible Underwear*
(sequel to *The Edible Woman* by Margaret Atwood)
Jamieson Wolf, Writer

Tyler gets me a job as a massage therapist, after that Tyler's pushing a mini-quiche in my mouth and saying, the first step to making up is you have to cry.

—From *Fight Club 2: Making Up*
(sequel to *Fight Club* by Chuck Palahniuk)
Scott Armstrong

"But Mitya," cried Ivan Karamazov, "the Father Zosima blintzes can retail at an even higher mark-up if you would only print the 'organic' label in English."

—From *The Brothers Karamazov, Part Deux: The California Years* (sequel to *The Brothers Karamazov* by Fyodor Dostoyevsky)
Anonymous

In a large cocktail shaker, mix: 3 parts premium tequila; 1 part Italian grapefruit soda; 1 fresh squeezed lime. Shake well, pour contents over ice into rocks glass.

—From *Tequila Mockingbird*
(sequel to *To Kill a Mockingbird* by Harper Lee)
Craig Herman, Philadelphia

Mrs Dalloway said she would buy the flour herself.

—From *Mrs Dalloway's Cookbook*
(sequel to *Mrs Dalloway* by Virginia Woolf)
Peter Mayer, Fiction Writer, New York City

My plums from the ice box are gone I am so hungry and all you left was a note? You couldn't have left just one plum?

—From *So What You Are Saying Is ...* (sequel to *This Is Just to Say* by William Carlos Williams)
Jeff Salane, New York City

Breathe air. Not too much.
Mostly oxygen.

—From *Air* (sequel to *In Defense of Food*
by Michael Pollan)
Damian Haas, Minneapolis

Why does every damned rich, famous person think they can
get into my restaurant without a reservation, just because
they are damned rich and famous and have eaten some
kinda offal at some point, huh?

—From *No Reservations? Fahgitaboutit!*
(sequel to *No Reservations* by Anthony Bourdain)
Gail Hutchison, Sexual Assault Services Coordinator,
Manteo, NC

You can stop playing now: everyone here is
more inclined toward love of food.

—From *Later on Twelfth Night*
(sequel to *Twelfth Night* by William Shakespeare)
Phil Lorenz

Scarlett was hungry.

—From *The Reconstruction of Scarlett* (sequel
to *Gone with the Wind* by Margaret Mitchell)
Robin Dennis, Flower Mound, TX

If you never eat alone, you can become a great networker; but if you never eat at all, you'll get thinner.

—From *Never Eat: Keith Ferrazi's Diet Book*
(sequel to *Never Eat Alone* by Keith Ferrazi)
Fern Reiss, AssociationofWriters.com

I had a restaurant in Albuquerque, at the foot of the Hyatt Regency.

—From *Out of Paprika*
(sequel to *Out of Africa* by Isak Dinesen)
Jack McKeown

PART XI

Weird, Wrong

"After Boo and all, I've since been attracted to mysterious men," Scout said before drawing on her cigarette, the glow lighting up the front porch steps.

—From *Boo's Legacy*
(sequel to *To Kill a Mockingbird* by Harper Lee)
Carol Hoenig, Writer, Publishing Consultant

Mistah Kurtz, he just wish he dead, last night drinkin gin like hippo drink swamp water.

—From *Liyer of Darkness*
(sequel to *Heart of Darkness* by Joseph Conrad)
John Maher, Foreign Service Officer

All of this happened while I was walking starving past a tattoo parlour in Christiana—and one should never walk past a tattoo parlour in a hungry delirium unless he wants it to leave its mark on him ...

—From *Hunger and Hungrier*
(sequel to *Hunger* by Knut Hamsun)
Lisa Morton, Bookseller, North Hollywood, CA

Harper Lee

"After Boo and all, I've since
been attracted to mysterious
men," Scout said before drawing
on her cigarette, the glow
lighting up the front porch steps.

He was Diddy, plain Diddy, in the morning, standing five feet eleven in one sneaker, he was P. Diddy in sequins, he was Sean John at school, he was Mr. Combs on the dotted line; but in my arms he was always Puffy.

—From *JLolita* (sequel to *Lolita* by Vladimir Nabokov)

Stan Friedman

In the town, there were two mutes and they were always texting one another.
—From *The Heart Was a Lonely Hunter* (sequel to *The Heart Is a Lonely Hunter* by Carson McCullers)
Ken Wohlrob, Writer, Brooklyn

It is not often that someone comes along who is friendly and tasty. Wilbur was both.
—From *Wilbur's Stockyard*
(sequel to *Charlotte's Web* by E. B. White)
Liz Frame, San Antonio, TX

Finally, it all made sense to Maurice; Clive must have been another creation of the Matrix, which explained the rather robotic lovemaking he had endured last Whitsunday Eve.
—From *Maurice: Revolutions*
(sequel to *Maurice* by E. M. Forster)
Michael Cornelius, Cambersburg, PA

The television was left on the from the night before and brown spittle stewed in a collection of plastic cups next to the sofa. The stereo system buzzed with the chatter of radio friendly rap-rock and several of my "brothers" had managed to find a place on the floor to sleep, content in their communal sweat and vomit. It was the beginning of Greek Week and we were destined for glory, love, and regret.

—From *Bloke House*
(sequel to *Bleak House* by Charles Dickens)
Anonymous

"Here's your rats!" said Winston as the rodents swarmed over O'Brien's bullet-ridden corpse, and smoke rose from the barrel of his Thompson submachine gun, the letters J-U-L-I-A carved into the stock.

—From *1985, by George Orwell and Frank Miller*
(sequel to *1984* by George Orwell)
Brian Yamauchi, Roboticist, Boston

Dr Benway, sweating slightly in the afternoon vapors, leaned into his medical bag, removed a much-used, slightly rusty forceps, dipped the instrument into the bag of heroin, just brought over the Himalayas by his trusty Mugwump castrato, Bogdacious, held the powder beneath his bulbous nose, smiled at his companion and said, "Here's looking at you, kid."

—From *Naked Afternoon Tea*
(sequel to *Naked Lunch* by William S. Burroughs)
Steve Adelson

Just as I was preparing to forge in the smithy of my soul the uncreated conscience of my race my cell phone rang. It was Warner Bros. offering half a mil for a polish on the "Terminator Salvation" script. Yes I said yes I will Yes.

—From *A Portrait of the Artist As an Old Hack* (sequel to *A Portrait of the Artist As a Young Man* by James Joyce)
Timothy Noah, Journalist

The screaming has become incessant across the sky. It has happened before, and now there is nothing to react to.

—From *Gravity's War*
(sequel to *Gravity's Rainbow* by Thomas Pynchon)
Jed Bickman

Revenge is de-lightful, it's de-licious, it's de-lovely!

—From *The De-Lovely Bones*
(sequel to *The Lovely Bones* by Alice Sebold)
Martin Masadao, Makati, Philippines

Just as I was preparing to forge in the smithy of my soul the uncreated conscience of my race my cell phone rang. It was Warner Bros. offering half a mil for a polish on the "Terminator Salvation" script. Yes I said yes I will Yes.

James Joyce

You are not the kind of baby who would go comatose after only one line of Bolivian Marching Powder.

—From *You and Me and Coma Baby Makes Three*
(sequel to *Bright Lights, Big City* by Jay McInerney)
Kevin Murphy

I knew I had seen her face years ago, as if in a dream, a cherub I once loved, but this nubile was not Lolita; it was her daughter.

—From *Run, Lolita, Run*
(sequel to *Lolita* by Vladimir Nabokov)
Antonio Fasciano, New York

It was a bright, cold day in April, and half of Russia was about to become radioactive.

—From *1984 III: 1986*
(sequel to *1984* by George Orwell)
Eric Weinstein

I was born ... several times. Once as a cute African American boy on a surprisingly smogless day in Gary, Indiana, then again, as a vaguely Caucasian dude sometime after Thriller came out, then again in the late nineties as a Welsh housewife, then in 2002 as pretty much a Frankensteinian miscellany.

—From *Peripheralsex: Something Happened to MJ*
(sequel to *Middlesex* by Jeffrey Eugenides)
David Eicke

As she pushed him under the wheels of the arriving train, she thought "I'll name him Anis—he would've liked that."

—From *Railroad Tracks Like Some Fairly Obvious Metaphor for a Way Out of an Unwanted Situation*
(sequel to *Hills Like White Elephants* by Ernest Hemingway)
Jason Westbrook, Student/Latin Teacher, Albuquerque, NM

And in the end, Man created God in His own image.

—From *The Newer Testament*
(sequel to *The Old Testament* by Various)
Edmund Glass

No and I said no meaning no with all my heart no when his wretched hands slithered across me like the warty toad found lurking in the fetid crease between the wall and the pavement moist from the continual damp and shade yet never able to sustain the merest hint of life let alone the delicacy of mountain flower or honest moss, and I asked myself how I ever once found something in the stumbling balding feckless—and what was that thing he carried round in his pocket all those years?—vision of man that I could ever attach sentiment or feeling or, my god yes, now that I recall the first time, yes passion, how could it ever have changed from that moment of pure vibrant spirit fused with feral perfume to this crabby dessicated scourge of an embrace in which he no longer knows how to touch me and I cannot even summon the will to be repulsed by him, no, no, please, no.

—From *Ulysses Returns*
(sequel to *Ulysses* by James Joyce)
Anonymous

Darlene wanted a big rack in the worst way, yet, no matter how often she called out D-cups from the Universe she woke every morning with the same sorry chicken-cutlet breasts and the creeping realization that The Secret was a simply a well-crafted lie.

—From *Trailer for Sale or Rent: Boob Job for 50 cents*
(sequel to *The Secret* by Rhonda Bryne)
Karen Spears Zacharias, Author, Oregon

PART XII

Tweets & Geeks

Fifty years later, firemen invent a new device called Twitter that lowers the burn temperature of books to 140 degrees. No one seemed to noti

—From *Fahrenheit 140*
(sequel to *Fahrenheit 451* by Ray Bradbury)
Peter Miller, Publishing

For thirty-five years now I've been in e-waste, and it's my indestructible heart.

—From *Too Quiet a Demise*
(sequel to *Too Loud a Solitude* by Bohumil Hrabal)
Paul Atwood

The public library was filled with the warm, crisp scent of freshly mowed grass as the afternoon sun cut through the windows and across the computer screen of my dearest friend, social networking and graphic design aficionado, Basil Hallward, who was beaming at his completion of the most striking page layout I had ever seen.

—From *The Myspace Page of Dorian Gray*
(sequel to *The Picture of Dorian Gray* by Oscar Wilde)
Megan Willan, Havre De Grace, MD

Mr. Jones, of the Manor Pharmacy, had locked the OxyContin and Vicodin up for the night, but was too affected by the diazepam to remember to shut the Demerol cabinet.

—From *Animal Pharmacy*
(sequel to *Animal Farm* by George Orwell)
Matt Schwartz, Book Marketer, New York City

The sky and the water were the color of 1's and 0's, and the sound you heard was white noise.

—From *Digital Neuromancer*
(sequel to *Neuromancer* by William Gibson)
Anonymous

The Martians regarded our world across the gulf of space, viewing their war machines, felled at the outskirts of our cities by humble germs, and with intellects vast and cool and unsympathetic, drew their plans for a far different and more insidious second invasion.

—From *War of the Inner Worlds*
(sequel to *War of the Worlds* by H. G. Wells)
Matthew Warner, Staunton, VA

He lay on the brown dirt, his chin on his folded arms, and high overhead the wind blew in the top of the cell phone tower.

—From *For Whom the iPhone Rings*
(sequel to *For Whom the Bell Tolls*
by Ernest Hemingway)
Mike Cassidy

And on the Eighth Day, God Googled.

—From *Exegesis*
(sequel to *The Bible (King James Version)*
by Many)
Evan Charkes

The sky was the color of a YouTube video, long since removed.

—From *Moll*
(sequel to *Neuromancer* by William Gibson)
Reuben Kabel

Sancho Panza looked at the forty or so windmills scattered across the Andalusian horizon, and then it hit him, maybe crazy old Don Quixote was right after all, the answer was so obvious that even his childish brain could grasp it: wind power would solve the world's energy crisis.

—From *Blowing in the Wind*
(sequel to *Don Quixote* by Miguel Cervantes)
Evan Charkes, New York

Now that you have mastered the recombinant DNA part, on to the implantation. ...

—From *Genetics for Dummies, Part Two* (sequel to *Genetics for Dummies* by Tara Rodd Robinson)
Jean Westcott, Book Marketing Manager, Northern Virginia

Where's Papa going with that Ethernet cable?

—From *Charlotte's Web Site*
(sequel to *Charlotte's Web* by E. B. White)
Michael Agger

In the End, God decided to hit the reset button.

—From *Yet Another Holy Book*
(sequel to *The Bible* by God et al.)
Kara Race-Moore

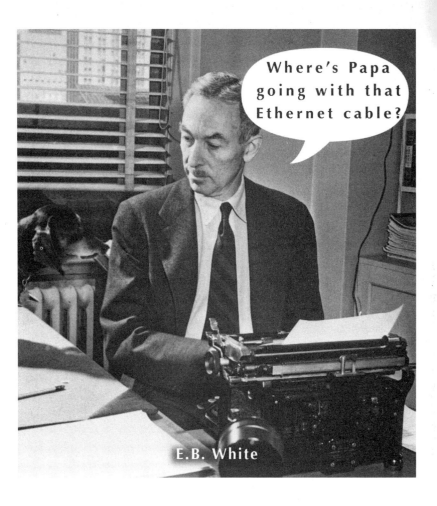

The seasons turn and change and once again A royal
Richard shines upon the world; Perchance you doubt my
parentage; then know That centuries from now my father's
blood Was analyzed and cloned and I was spawned; And
from that future time I made escape; For I am sworn to right
the ancient wrong: I will supplant, though no man knows it
yet, This Tudor house with our Plantagenet.

—From *Richard IV*
(sequel to *Richard III* by William Shakespeare)
Norman Szabo, Taiwan ROC

This isn't a palimpsest of my palimpsest.
—From *The Handmaid's Tweet*
(sequel to *The Handmaid's Tale* by Margaret Atwood)
Martin Masadao, Makati, Philippines

That was when I saw the light: in a side-by-side comparison,
even the Panthéon's majestic 67-m pendulum was
completely outperformed by the most basic sat-nav.

—From *Foucault's GPS*
(sequel to *Foucault's Pendulum* by Umberto Eco)
Norman Szabo, Taiwan, ROC

73X7 m3h 15HM3al

—From *mo8Y d1CK 11 (The L33T edition)*
(sequel to *Moby Dick* by Herman Melville)
Frank Laycock

Alice was beginning to get very tired of waiting in line with her BFF at the Apple Genius Bar: once or twice she had peeped into the Kindle her BFF was reading, but it had no pictures in it, "and what is the use of an e-book," thought Alice, "without pictures?"

—From *Alice's Adventures in Second Life* (sequel to *Alice's Adventures in Wonderland* by Lewis Carroll)
Lauren Gilbert, Librarian, Huntington, NY

Finn Fogg held his breath and clicked the mouse; it was his first attempt to achieve teleportation.

—From *Around the World in Eight Seconds* (sequel to *Around the World in Eighty Days* by Jules Verne)
A. F. Stewart, Author

In the distant future, Frederic, realizing that he was somehow no longer a French dandy, but instead a heavily armed cyborg knee-deep in gristle, shrapnel and unidentified limbs, accepted that the time for idleness and romance had passed—now it was time for payback.

—From *The Death of Sentiment* (sequel to *Sentimental Education* by Gustave Flaubert)
Drew Toal

When the power surge wiped his hard drive, destroying the only copy of his manuscript, Bastian Balthazar Bux rued the fact that he had neglected to back it up.

—From *The Prematurely Ended Story*
(sequel to *The Neverending Story* by Michael Ende)
Caitlin Fawcett

Now is the winter of our discontent—Oh wait, I feel much better.

—From *Richard the Third on Zoloft*
(sequel to *Richard III* by William Shakespeare)
Daniel Gallant, New York

"All art is quite useless," I thought as I once again used the airbrush tool smoothing away the wrinkles at the corner of my right eye.

—From *The Photoshopping of Dorian Gray*
(sequel to *The Picture of Dorian Gray* by Oscar Wilde)
Evan Schwartz, Philadelphia

There once was a man named Milo who never had enough change for the tolls—not just sometimes, but always.

—From *The Phantom E-ZPass Lane*
(sequel to *The Phantom Tollbooth* by Norton Juster)
Stephanie Anderson, Bookseller, Brooklyn

```
Text me Ishmael
(ISH@aol.com).
```
—From *Moby II: Much Information*
(sequel to *Moby Dick* by Herman Melville)
Jack Nnessel, Bookseller (Rare And Collectible),
New York City

If you really want to hear about it, take that stupid helmet off.

—From *The Catcher in Space*
(sequel to *The Catcher in the Rye* by J. D. Salinger)
Brittany Pogue-Mohammed

You have a friend request from God. Confirm
as Friend or Ignore?

—From *Facebook of Common Prayer*
(sequel to *Book of Common Prayer*
by Thomas Cranmer)
Lauren Gilbert, Librarian, Huntington, NY

Robert Langdon stared at the 500-year-old bank book from
Milan's venerable Banca di Tutti Lire, stunned by its
implications: Leonardo's vast fortune was intact and
available for withdrawal from any ATM, provided one had
the Master's PIN.

—From *The Da Vinci PIN Code*
(sequel to *The Da Vinci Code* by Dan Brown)
Larry Hughes, Book Flack At Large

"WUU2? NMH" Me Alex & 3 BFFS Jaden
Caden & Trip mkg plans 2nite TTUL bro
PAW

—From *A Digital Orange*
(sequel to *A Clockwork Orange* by Anthony Burgess)
Laura Martineau, Grant Writer, Connecticut

Unfortunately, we had not counted on the Martians' developing vaccines.

—From *War of the Worlds II: Revenge of the Martians*
(sequel to *War of the Worlds* by H. G. Wells)
Emma Joyce

`I twit a tweet of myself.`

—From *the sequel to Song of Myself*
by Walt Whitman
Anonymous

Call me, Ishmael.

—From *Mobile Dick*
(sequel to *Moby Dick* by David Weinberger)
David Weinberger

Do androids tweet electric sheep?

—From *Androids of Twitter*
(sequel to *Do Androids Dream of Electric Sheep?*
by Philip K. Dick)
Marilyn Peake, Author

(

Rumors of my death
had been greatly exaggerated.

—From *The Book Strikes Back*
(sequel to *Book: The Sequel* by Book)
Anonymous

ABOUT *BOOK: THE SEQUEL*

This book is the product of many talented hands working together in ways both old and new.

It was written between April 28 and May 28, 2009, by readers, writers, and other book lovers the world over. The contributions were culled from hundreds of submissions to www.bookthesequel.com. The contributors come from all walks of life, from all over the United States, and from places as far apart from each other as England, New Zealand, the Philippines, and Japan. One thing they all share is the love of a great book.

The Perseus Books Group challenged itself and its business partners in the industry to use the notion of "what comes next?" for favorite characters and stories as a springboard for an experiment in "what comes next?" in publishing. With that in mind, *Book: The Sequel* was edited, designed, laid out, and produced in a wide variety of formats (i.e., print, audio, large text, and e-book) in forty-eight hours on May 28–29, 2009, at Book Expo America in New York City, the annual convention of the U.S. book industry.

While none of us know exactly what the future holds for

the book business, we have some strong hunches about the future of publishing, which have been underscored in the making of this book:

- *More formats:* Books will be available where, when, and how readers want them—print, e-books on various platforms, digital audio, large print, and more.
- *More collaboration:* Publishing has always been a team effort, and the team is growing—over twenty companies participated in this effort.
- *More connected:* "The book" and "the conversation about the book" are more pervasively connected, on Facebook, on Twitter, on literary blogs, in other reader communities, among librarians, at retailer sites, and, yes, in hallways, by water coolers, and over lunches.
- *Faster to market:* Writing a book can happen slowly (twenty years for a novel like Katherine Anne Porter's *Ship of Fools*) or (quickly for a book like this one), but bringing that book to the public is likely to be much more efficient today.

And while changes in book form and publishing approaches are both inevitable and in many ways welcome, we believe a good read is eternal. In that spirit, royalties from *Book: The Sequel* are being donated to The National Book Foundation, presenter of the National Book Awards.

So enjoy *Book: The Sequel*—and whether you are reading a printed book, listening to it on headphones, or experiencing it digitally, you are helping write the story of What Comes Next.

ACKNOWLEDGMENTS

The Perseus Books Group would like to thank the following people and organizations

Audible.com
The Book Report Network
The Caravan Project
Barnes & Noble.com
Corbis
DailyLit
The eBook Store
Edwards Brothers
eMusic
Expanded Books
Lightning Source

North Plains Systems
On Demand Books
OverDrive
ReadHowYouWant
Reading Group Choices
Rick's Image Works
SharedBook
Sony
University Press
   Audiobooks, LLC
Verso Reader Channels